Torque brims with excitement perfect for thrill-seekers of all kinds. Discover daring survival skills, explore uncharted worlds, and marvel at mighty engines and extreme sports. In *Torque* books, anything can happen. Are you ready?

This edition first published in 2024 by Bellwether Media, Inc.

No part of this publication may be reproduced in whole or in part without written permission of the publisher. For information regarding permission, write to Bellwether Media, Inc., Attention: Permissions Department, 6012 Blue Circle Drive, Minnetonka, MN 55343.

Library of Congress Cataloging-in-Publication Data

LC record for Apache Helicopter available at: https://lccn.loc.gov/2023047017

Text copyright © 2024 by Bellwether Media, Inc. TORQUE and associated logos are trademarks and/or registered trademarks of Bellwether Media, Inc.

Editor: Kieran Downs   Designer: Jeffrey Kollock

Printed in the United States of America, North Mankato, MN.

TABLE OF CONTENTS

A FLYING TANK	4
WHAT IS THE APACHE HELICOPTER?	6
A FIGHTING MACHINE	10
APACHES FLY INTO THE FUTURE	18
APACHE HELICOPTER FACTS	20
GLOSSARY	22
TO LEARN MORE	23
INDEX	24

★ A FLYING TANK

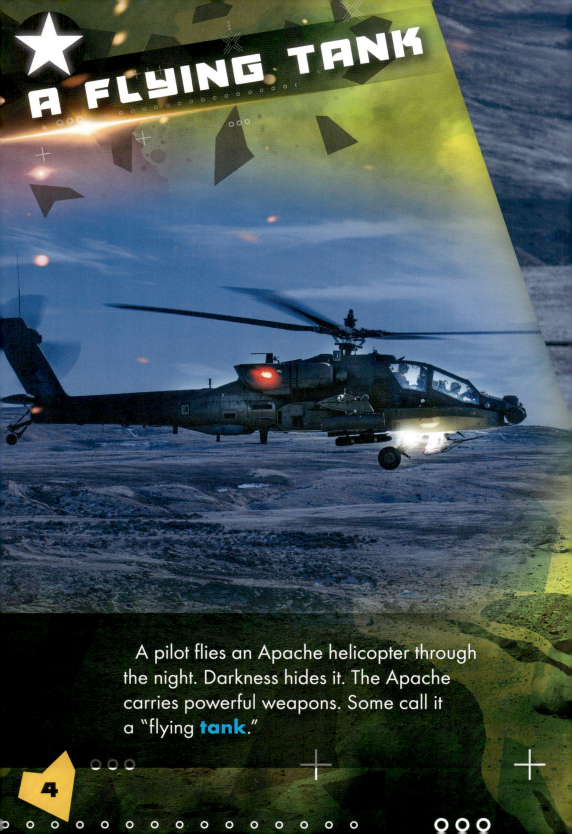

A pilot flies an Apache helicopter through the night. Darkness hides it. The Apache carries powerful weapons. Some call it a "flying **tank**."

4

The pilot guides the aircraft to hide behind a hill. Enemy tanks are waiting on the far side of the hill. The Apache fires at the tanks. Its shots are guided by **laser beams**. Targets hit! Another mission is done!

WHAT IS THE APACHE HELICOPTER?

The Apache is a United States Army attack helicopter. It has been used since 1984.

The Apache is built for **combat**. It is loaded with rockets, **missiles**, and a **cannon**. It destroys tanks and **armored** trucks. It sees the enemy's location and sends that information to troops on the ground. The Apache also fights other helicopters.

MISSILE

Apaches have been used in many missions. They were key in Operation Desert Storm in 1991. They helped the Army destroy Iraq's tanks and weapons.

APACHES AROUND THE WORLD

The U.S. is not the only military with Apaches. Countries such as Egypt, Israel, and Japan fly them, too!

Later, U.S. troops used Apaches in 1992 in Operation Restore Hope. In this mission, troops flew Apaches to help keep peace in Somalia. In 2002, U.S. troops used Apaches against **al Qaeda** fighters in Afghanistan during Operation Anaconda.

MISSIONS MAP

A FIGHTING MACHINE

APACHE PRODUCTION LINE

EARLY APACHE

During the **Vietnam War**, U.S. helicopters did not have strong weapons. They did not have armor to protect pilots. After the war, the Army worked to create a fighting helicopter. They invented the Apache. The Army started using them in 1984.

SIZE CHART

LENGTH
48.16 FEET (14.68 METERS)

HEIGHT
15.49 FEET (4.72 METERS)

ROTOR DIAMETER
48 FEET (14.63 METERS)

The first Apaches were called the AH-64A. The newest Apaches are called the AH-64E.

11

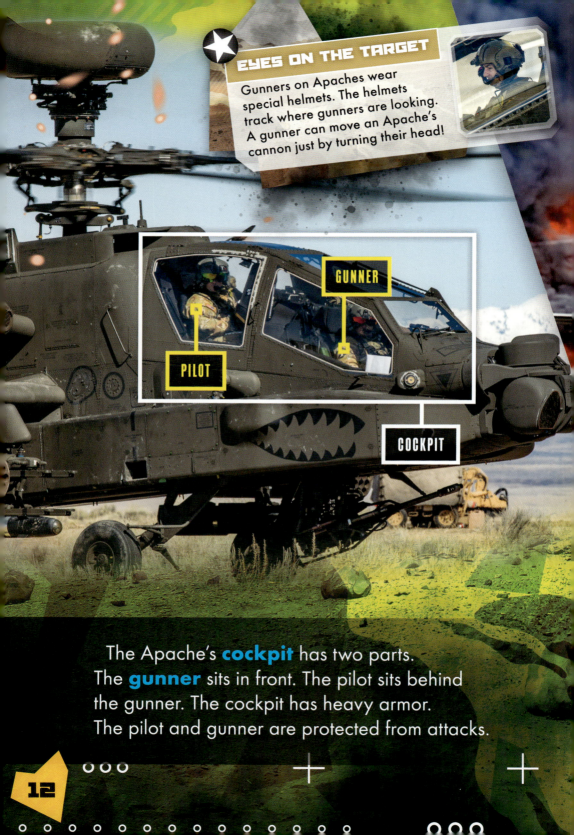

EYES ON THE TARGET

Gunners on Apaches wear special helmets. The helmets track where gunners are looking. A gunner can move an Apache's cannon just by turning their head!

PILOT

GUNNER

COCKPIT

The Apache's **cockpit** has two parts. The **gunner** sits in front. The pilot sits behind the gunner. The cockpit has heavy armor. The pilot and gunner are protected from attacks.

12

The Apache has special **radar**. It helps the crew spot enemies. In daylight, the crew sees with a camera. **Sensors** help them see in the dark, rain, or fog.

RADAR

SENSORS

The Apache has twin **turbine engines**. It also has **filters** to protect the engines from sand and dust. The helicopter flies forward, backward, and sideways. It can also **hover**. It hides behind hills and attacks enemies.

FILTER

TURBINE ENGINE

APACHE HOVERING

HOW AN APACHE HIDES

1 A scout helicopter aims at the target with laser beams

LASER

2 The Apache fires missiles while hidden behind a hill

LASER-GUIDED MISSILE

3 Missiles follow the laser to hit the target

The Apache can fly close to the ground. It can travel up to 173 miles (278 kilometers) per hour! Its fast speeds help it surprise enemies.

The Apache's main weapon is Hellfire missiles. It can carry up to 16 Hellfire missiles at once. These missiles can burn through tank armor.

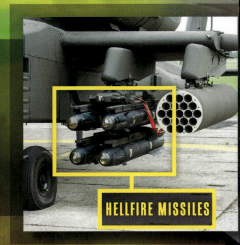

HELLFIRE MISSILES

PARTS OF AN APACHE HELICOPTER

- TURBINE ENGINE
- RADAR
- ROTORS
- COCKPIT
- HYDRA ROCKET LAUNCHER
- HELLFIRE MISSILE
- CANNON
- SENSORS

16

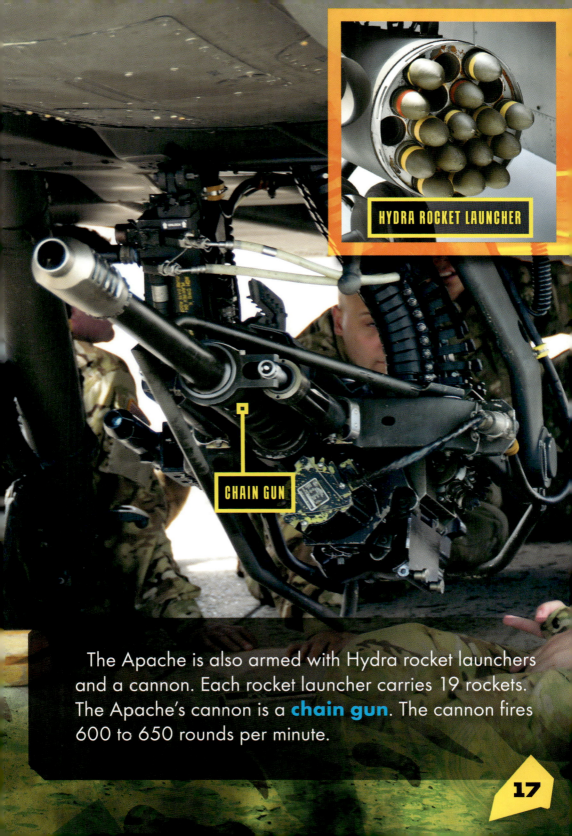

HYDRA ROCKET LAUNCHER

CHAIN GUN

The Apache is also armed with Hydra rocket launchers and a cannon. Each rocket launcher carries 19 rockets. The Apache's cannon is a **chain gun**. The cannon fires 600 to 650 rounds per minute.

APACHES FLY INTO THE FUTURE

The U.S. Army plans to improve the Apache. Better engines will give it more power. It will also be able to fly further.

Improved sensors will help its crew see enemies better. Better weapons will be able to hit targets more easily. Apaches will be the U.S. Army's combat helicopter for years to come!

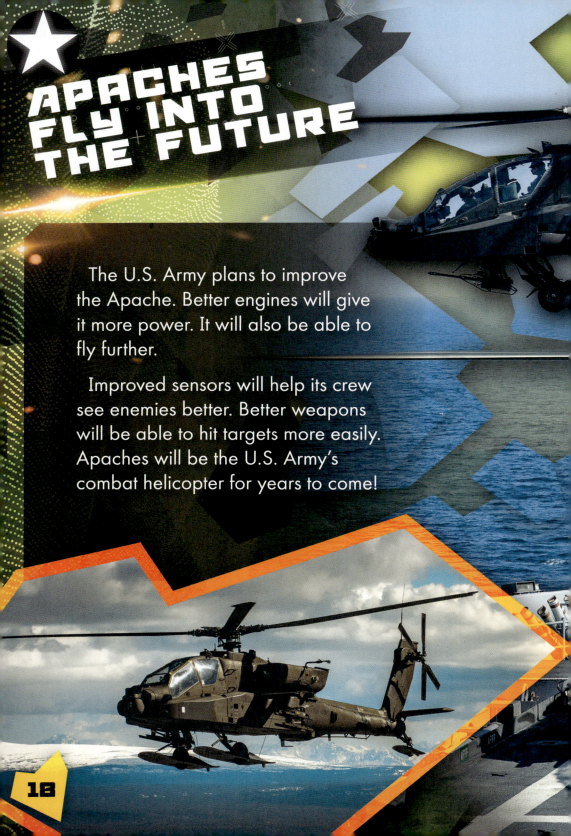

APACHE HELICOPTER FACTS

STATS

TOP SPEED

173 miles
(278 kilometers)
per hour

RANGE

299 miles
(481 kilometers)

ALTITUDE CEILING

20,000 feet
(6,096 meters)

20

WEAPONS

16 MISSILES

76 ROCKETS

1,200 CHAIN GUN ROUNDS

MANUFACTURER

Boeing

BRANCH OF THE MILITARY

U.S. Army

MAIN PURPOSE

combat

CLASS

TWIN-ENGINE ATTACK HELICOPTER

CREW

2

OPERATION

MORE THAN **1,275** APACHE HELICOPTERS IN USE TODAY

FIRST YEAR USED

1984

21

GLOSSARY

al Qaeda—a terrorist group; terrorists are people who use violence and fear to try to get something.

armored—covered in thick plates for protection

cannon—a large gun

chain gun—a type of gun that uses a motor to fire

cockpit—the place in an aircraft where the crew sits

combat—a fight between armed forces

filters—devices that protect engines from sand and dirt

gunner—a crew member who fires the guns

hover—to stay in one spot while in flight

laser beams—narrow, bright beams of light

missiles—explosives that are sent to targets

radar—a device that uses energy waves to sense and see objects

sensors—devices that detect objects and send that information to a computer

tank—an armored vehicle that moves on two belts with wheels inside them; tanks are able to move over rough land.

turbine engines—engines that spin to power the helicopter

Vietnam War—a war in Southeast Asia that took place from 1955 to 1975; U.S. troops fought in the war from 1965 to 1973.

TO LEARN MORE

AT THE LIBRARY

Brody, Walt. *How Military Helicopters Work*. Minneapolis, Minn.: Lerner Publications, 2020.

McKinney, Donna. *V-22 Osprey*. Minneapolis, Minn.: Bellwether Media, 2024.

Schuh, Mari. *Military Aircraft*. North Mankato, Minn.: Pebble, 2022.

ON THE WEB

FACTSURFER

Factsurfer.com gives you a safe, fun way to find more information.

1. Go to www.factsurfer.com

2. Enter "Apache helicopter" into the search box and click 🔍.

3. Select your book cover to see a list of related content.

INDEX

Afghanistan, 9
Apache helicopter facts, 20–21
armor, 6, 10, 12, 16
camera, 13
cannon, 6, 7, 12, 17
cockpit, 12
combat, 6, 18
crew, 12, 13, 18
enemies, 5, 6, 13, 14, 15, 18
filters, 14
future, 18
gunner, 12
helmets, 12
history, 6, 8, 9, 10, 11
hover, 14
how an Apache hides, 15
Iraq, 8
laser beams, 5
map, 9
missiles, 6, 16
missions, 5, 8, 9
name, 4, 11
parts of an Apache helicopter, 16
pilot, 4, 5, 10, 12
radar, 13
rockets, 6, 17
sensors, 13, 18
size, 11
Somalia, 9
speed, 15
turbine engines, 14, 18
United States Army, 6, 8, 9, 10, 18
Vietnam War, 10
weapons, 4, 6, 7, 8, 10, 12, 16, 17, 18

The images in this book are reproduced through the courtesy of: Ruediger Hess/ DVIDS, cover; Cameron Roxberry/ DVIDS, pp. 3, 18; Kyle Abraham/ DVIDS, pp. 4, 5, 12, 14 (filter); Mike Harvey/ Wikimedia Commons, p. 6; Avpics/ Alamy, pp. 7, 16; Katherine Milberry/ DVIDS, p. 8; Robert D. Ward/ Wikimedia Commons, p. 10 (inset); Aviation History Collection/ Alamy, 10; Eve Baker/ DVIDS, p. 12 (fun fact); Andrew Harker, p. 13; Travis Mueller/ DVIDS, p. 13 (sensors); Gary Stedman/ Alamy, p. 14; rlat, p. 16 (missiles); Charles Rosemond/ DVIDS, p. 17; PikaPower, p. 17 (Hydra); Jon Rasmussen/ DVIDS, p. 19; fotorobs, p. 20; Erich Backes/ DVIDS, p. 23.

24